Around Here

Around Here

Poems by

J.R. Solonche

© 2022 J.R. Solonche. All rights reserved.
This material may not be reproduced in any form, published,
reprinted, recorded, performed, broadcast,
rewritten or redistributed without
the explicit permission of J.R. Solonche.
All such actions are strictly prohibited by law.

Cover design by Shay Culligan

ISBN: 978-1-63980-210-4

Kelsay Books
502 South 1040 East, A-119
American Fork, Utah 84003
Kelsaybooks.com

Books by This Author

The Lost Notebook of Zhao Li
It's about Time
The Book of a Small Fisherman
Coming To
Life-Size
The Five Notebooks of Zhao Li
Selected Poems 2002-2021
Years Later
The Dust
A Guide of the Perplexed
For All I Know
The Moon Is the Capital of the World
Piano Music
Enjoy Yourself
The Time of Your Life
The Porch Poems
To Say the Least
A Public Place
True Enough
If You Should See Me Walking on the Road
I, Emily Dickinson and Other Found Poems
The Jewish Dancing Master
Tomorrow, Today and Yesterday
In Short Order
Invisible
Heart's Content
Won't Be Long
Beautiful Day
Peach Girl: Poems for a Chinese Daughter (with Joan I. Siegel)

Contents

Part I

Around Here	15
Country Cemetery in the Snow	16
In the Monastery	17
Miracles	18
The Last Words of My Father	19
What to Make	20
There Is Something to Be Learned	21
The Shadows	22
An Owl Is Calling	23
Women	24
Turner	25
Why	26
Eleven Short Pastorals	27
Twenty Poems Beginning with Lines by Emily Dickinson	31
March 14	36
March 20	37
My Neighbor's Wheelbarrow	38
Two of My Neighbors	39
Edward Hopper, *Seven A.M., 1948*	40
Edward Hopper, *Last Gas*	41
Edward Hopper, *Automat*	42
Edward Hopper, *Solitude*	43
Edward Hopper, *Entrance to a City*	44
Edward Hopper, *Sunlight in an Empty Room*	45
Edward Hopper, *Nighthawks*	46
Teaching	47
The Singer in the Bar	48
On the First Day of the Wild Cherry's Blossoming	49
Falcon	50
I Have Often Thought	51

Part II Ghazal-Sonnets

Swan   55
Wolf   56
Beard   57
Letter   58
Bridge   59
Woman   60
Face   61
Fame   62
Money   63
Sleep   64
Paper   65
Nose   66
Time   67
Star   68
Corn   69
Chair   70
Bed   71
Hair   72
Foot   73
Hope   74
Work   75
Wedding   76
Answer   77
Journey   78
Truth   79
Nonsense   80
Mask   81
Light   82
Owl   83
Wheel   84
Bell   85

Fool	86
Laugh(ter)	87
Shit	88
Morning	89
Luck	90
Silence	91
Smoke	92
Blood	93
Ghost	94
Peace	95
Lightning	96
Weather	97
School	98
Home	99
Miracle	100

Part I

Around Here

Around here is no different
from around anywhere.

Our trees are no different
and are no differently bare.

Our lake, no different
from any one-mile long lake,

is frozen over no differently
with ice of no difference.

My neighbors around here
are the same as anywhere.

Even the widow and her dog
are the same as everywhere.

Nevertheless, of any way
I could, I walk their way,

which is the only way
that makes any difference.

Country Cemetery in the Snow

After years lying on their backs,
someone has stood up the stones.
No doubt, someone from the town.
It doesn't matter, though, whether
upright or flat on the ground.
They can't be read anyway. The
names and dates are worn away
into the oblivion where the family
is gone, the one oblivion there is.
But it was a nice gesture, a kindly
gesture by someone from the town
to keep their heads above the snow.

In the Monastery

First Student:
The Master talks a lot.

Second Student:
Yes, he does koan and on.

Miracles

I don't believe in them,
no, not for a minute.
But I'll tell you what a miracle is.
A miracle is a poem
by William Carlos Williams called
"The Crimson Cyclamen,"
which I have read many times
and never tire of reading,
and each time it is the miracle of the rock
giving forth wine,
the miracle of the dead rising to speak.

The Last Words of My Father

I don't know what they were.
I wasn't there in the hospital.
But knowing my father,
he would not have said anything.
He was a taciturn man.
I know only what he wrote
in the note he left for my mother,
for she told me what it said.
It said, "I don't have enough money
for a taxi. I'm taking the bus to the hospital."

What to Make

What to make
of this February thaw?

A hawk whistles
its answer from the top

of the ash tree
where two crows

have nothing nice
to say about it.

There Is Something to Be Learned

There is something to be learned
from watching the ice melt,
return to the water it was before it froze.
It might have to do with wisdom
or something to do with change,
which some say is the same as wisdom.

The Shadows

The shadows of things
make figures
on the snow
between the footprints
the wildlife prefigured there.

An Owl Is Calling

An owl is calling.
I hear him calling from out there across the lake.
I wait for his mate to answer.
I wait. I wait. I wait.
Now she answers.
Now I exhale.
Now I can go in.

Women

I met the widow Thaler.
She looked great.
You look great, I said.
She laughed.
I didn't laugh.
Tell me, I said.
Are you having something with your neighbor?
I pointed to his house.
Yes, she said.
We're good friends.
Then she kissed me on the mouth.
So this is why I'll never understand women.

Turner

Before I saw the movie, *Mr. Turner,*
I wanted to be van Gogh,
but since seeing the movie *Mr. Turner,*
I want to be Turner,
for what better way to live
than to be lashed to the mast
of a ship in a snow squall,
and what better way to die
than with "The sun is God" on your lips?

Why

"Why do I write today?"
This is what you asked, Bill,
and you answered it clearly,
cleanly, calmly, with precise
beauty and beautiful precision (yes,
they are different, you laugh!)
I, too, ask, "Why do I write today?"
and I, too, answer but only with
the imprecision and ugliness
of the great terrible "Because."

Eleven Short Pastorals

1.

"Spare me the puns!"
he shouted upwardly
at the crow overhead crowing
in the middle of the tail wind in its tail,
crowning itself king of the sky.

2.

The sun hungers,
so wakes from its fast,
so eats the snow for lunch,
so when he offers it himself so laughs, "Not yet."

3.

Smell it almost,
the wind most of all,
for it is the wind that has something
of the spring in it,
the fresh full of sweetness
that the once and forever spring
makes from the leaf and ditch decay
of winter's dirt, sweeter than death.

4.

The March snow is wet
and heavy and
drops from the sky's tired hands.

5.

The focus is the sun
as the sun focuses its expertise
on the job at hand.
"Concentrate," it burns into the earth's brow—
for what millionth time?—
"Remember how to rejoice!"

6.

On the road,
three white cars—
one—then another—then another—
three in a row,
spaced minutes apart.
This is the snow melting into the black river.

7.

A welcome sight:
the table on the patio,
none the worse for wearing
ice and snow,
and the blue chair
that the sun has been sitting in
and warming up for me,
and the breeze that tosses
a page or two
just enough to remind me
who out here the boss is.

8.

A fly, the first called forth
by the sun I've seen,
answers with itself,
soundless, without a buzz,
which, perhaps it has yet to learn.

9.

I see it,
the work that has to be done.
I see the posts
that have to be pulled up,
the fencing around them having been
removed in the fall.
I see the dead growth,
lanky, falling over itself, awkward.

I see how the big planters
will need to be stained again.
I see how bald
the ground is under the magnolia tree.
It will take a lot of topsoil
and seed to take care of that.
I see it.

10.

Should you add a figure?
Do what the painters do?
For the sake of scale?

For the good of the human solely?
No, only this—
the wild cherry tree only
smack dab in the center,
and the woodpecker back behind you,
the one you can hear
but cannot see.

11.

The ice melts,
and along with it the snow,
both rushing together as one downhill
and through the culvert
under the driveway, rushing,
impatient, to the lake,
and there, then over the spillway
into the brook, taking in all the others
from all around it,
adding the song of each to a loud unison,
and finally to the river,
which hushes all to silence and patience,
and the ocean, and the patient silence that is the ocean.

Twenty Poems Beginning with Lines by Emily Dickinson

1.

The fingers of the light
grow heavy on my lids.
I say, "Hurry" to the night.
"Here is where I'm hid."

2.

The life that tied too tight escapes
its bonds, but knows not where to go.
It flees from light of day, gropes
through dark of night, repeating, "Oh, oh, oh."

3.

The loneliness one dare not sound
is the heart's best loneliness,
the loneliness that can't be found
in any other of the world's recesses.

4.

The only news I know
is all the news of all the days
of all the worlds ago
which came about but yesterday.

5.

The most pathetic thing I do
is what I'm doing now,
one hand scribbling blue,
the other holding up my brow.

6.

The most important population
is the one that's not yet born,
for that will be the only nation
ours has not yet seen to scorn.

7.

The opening and the close.
Ditto.
That's all there is, I suppose.
Don't you know?

8.

The pile of years is not so high
that I can't climb it every day,
and at the top, I breathe a sigh,
then climb down the same way.

9.

In other motes
I have no interest.
Only my own floats
to float me best.

10.

Not any sunny tune
can cheer me
when I am down.
Then only the blues completes me.

11.

The past is such a curious creature.
It comes and goes so magically in the mind.
Disappearance is its primary feature,
and when you face it, it's already behind.

12.

The riddle we can guess
is not the worthy one.
Only if we are powerless
can we say the answer's won.

13.

The mountain sat upon the plain.
It looked so heavy sitting there,
but the land did not complain.
It made less sound than my chair.

14.

The way hope builds his house,
you'd think he knew his business.
The walls are straight, the roof is tight,
but, oh, there's no foundation under it.

15.

The outer from the inner
is often difficult to tell,
and especially for a sinner
does it never go too well.

16.

Oh shadow on the grass,
why did you frighten me so?
I knew you will quickly pass
by as usual. Yes, I knew. I know.

17.

Trust in the unexpected.
It will never disappoint,
for when you think the future is dead,
it comes as though bidden to anoint.

18.

Impossibility like wine
gets better after years.
The passing time makes fine
what once were certainty's tears.

19.

The stars are old that stood for me.
Their eyes are weak, their hair all gray.
They've done their years of duty,
so let them go their quiet way.

20.

Look back on time with kindly eyes
though time looks cruelly on you.
It took so long to make you wise,
don't waste what little yet is due.

March 14

Today is Einstein's birthday,
and the sun is still shining
just as it was when I wrote this
the first time last year.

March 20

Before the flowers
sound,
the sounds flower.

Across the road,
in the woods, birds,
hidden among

the trees. How many?
Hundreds? It sounds
like hundreds

of birds hidden
among the trees
in the woods

across the road.
Listen. This
is the flower

I mean, the one
with feathers,
the flying one,

that of the maiden
called spring
is so fast to first deflower.

My Neighbor's Wheelbarrow

is red, like the famous one,
and I suppose a lot depends on it,
like the famous one,
and the rainwater will glisten the same
as on the famous one,
and his chickens are white,
like the famous ones,
but that still does not excuse
the mess they make of the mulch
around my wild cherry tree.

Two of My Neighbors

are flying the Gadsden Flag,
the one designed by Colonel
Christopher Gadsden of South
Carolina in 1775, which he
presented to the American navy,
which shows a timber rattlesnake
with thirteen rattles coiled to strike
on a yellow field with the words,
"Don't Tread on Me." You would
think one of them at least would
know that you can't tread on
something ten feet off the ground.

Edward Hopper, *Seven A.M., 1948*

The edge of the building
marks the end of the town,

the edge of the woods.
A store. But what kind?

The bottles in the window.
Beer or hair tonic?

And the advertisements.
What are they advertising?

The center is the clock.
It is central to the end.

As is its shadow.
As is time.

And its shadow.

Edward Hopper, *Last Gas*

Even the three redheaded
sisters turn away.

Even the winged horse
cannot save us now.

Edward Hopper, *Automat*

The reflection of the lights
in the window above the head

of the woman, solitary,
solidly in the center,

whose face says, "Far away,
far, far away," must be

the road on which she has,
a few moments ago, arrived,

or if not, it must be the road on which
she will, as soon as the cup,

a few moments from now,
is empty, surely depart.

Edward Hopper, *Solitude*

A road with no signs.
A house with no drive.
An horizon with no features.

The grass, uncut around the house,
as tall as the grass everywhere.
No smoke from the chimney.

But the shades are drawn
to the same level in the windows.
So someone must be there.

Or must have been.
And the road must lead
somewhere. Or must have led to the sea.

To the city. Must go somewhere.
Or must have gone.
Somewhere else to be alone.

Edward Hopper, *Entrance to a City*

It is filled with his sunlight.
(Sunlight like no other.)

Off-white, off-yellow, pale, flushed,
flat, sandblasted.

It has his dark corner.
(Dark corner like no other.)

In this case, the lower left hand.
Not gothic, not mysterious, not sexual.

The tunnel the railroad tracks from the country
disappear into, the non-descript side-entrance to hell.

Edward Hopper, *Sunlight in an Empty Room*

With no figure illumined in it,
reading a letter or pouring milk
from a pitcher or playing a lute
or only blankly staring down
at the floor, shall we say that
the subject is the sunlight?
And what of the landscape through
the window that is no landscape at all,
but what appears to be a single tree,
its leaves brushing against the house?
And with this mere corner of sky,
why did he bother with it at all?
Perhaps we have it wrong.
Perhaps it is not the sunlight
that's the subject, but the room,
or the shadows that are most
of the room, or the shape of light on
the wall in the center that looks like a door.

Edward Hopper, *Nighthawks*

I don't wonder about them really,
the four in the coffee shop,
the nighthawks (if you count
the short-order cook as a nighthawk),
the man with his back to us, absorbed
in his own thoughts, or listening
to the conversation between the couple
and the short-order cook. I wonder
about the family up there in that
apartment above their own restaurant
across the street, in bed on this hot
summer night with the windows open.
I wonder about the wife, who is
sobbing silently to herself, thinking
about the boyfriend who jilted her
back in high school because the man
with his back to us reminds her of him.
I wonder about the husband, who is
smiling silently to himself because he
is having a wet dream about the redhead.
I wonder about the teenaged daughter,
who is now, in minute detail,
planning her escape.

Teaching

Teaching, too, is labor. Everyday
to be up to the task, everyday
the master of a hundred worlds,
of casual words, and of causal words,
to confront the faces added to or taken
from. Do you know when you add a
thought there, it shows in the eyes,
it shows in the mouth's subtle creases?
Do you know, when you stop a thought,
when you turn it aside with a straight
line, with the shortest distance from there
to here, it shows in the brow's labor?
Exhaustion. Do you know that teaching
is exhaustion, everyday reaching out for
youth's heavy hope, and your own
always holding, putting nothing down?
Teaching, too, is aching shoulders and back,
tired arms, legs, a heart's hard work.

The Singer in the Bar

The singer in the bar
has three guitars.
One is brown.
One is white.
One is red.
None is blue.

The singer in the bar
isn't very good.
Not on brown.
Not on white.
Not on red.
At least he doesn't have a blue.

It must be understood
that it doesn't matter to the patrons
in the bar
drinking beer
that the singer
isn't very good.

On the First Day of the Wild Cherry's Blossoming

On the first day of the wild
cherry's blossoming,
I stand beneath it,
looking up at the branches,
while it is still more sky
than branches,
at the first shy color
just shy of color,
and I close my eyes.
In my mind I try to become
a wild cherry tree on
the first day of its blossoming.
And when I open them,
all I see are tears.

Falcon

She is the finished business of flight.
She is the throwing knife perfectly balanced in the sky's palm.

She is the thought of the falconer before he thinks it.
She is the daughter of the valley and the wind.

She is the arrow that returns to the quiver.
She is the edge keened on the whetstone of her ancestors.

She is the goddess it does no good to worship.
She is the lightning with feathers.

She is the shadow with claws.
She is the eye with wings.

She is the death wish of the mourning dove.
She is the merciful needle.

I Have Often Thought

I have often thought
of what I want
to be doing when death comes.

When I was young,
I wanted to die
in a battle,

a righteous war against evil,
a hero's death,
a banner in my hand

and a bullet through the heart.
Later I thought
it would be better

to die in bed, of old age,
taken from life
in the middle of sleep,

dreamless into dreamlessness.
Now I want to die
sitting in a chair

very much like this chair,
by a window very much
like this window,

a worn yellow pencil
in my hand
very much like this

worn yellow pencil in my hand,
writing a poem like this one.
neither very good nor very bad,

Part II
Ghazal-Sonnets

Swan

Old English *swan* "swan," from Proto-Germanic "swanaz," Old
 Saxon
swan, Old Norse svanr, Danish svane, Middle Dutch "swane."

A wonderful book is E.B. White's *The Trumpet of the Swan.*
A great fairy tale is about the ugly duckling that becomes a swan.

Another Andersen literary fairy tale is "The Wild Swans."
Swans native to Australia are black swans.

Native to South America are black-necked swans.
A group of wild swans is a *herd,* a *fleet,* a group of captive swans.

The coscoroba of South America is not considered a true swan.
The British Monarch retains the right to ownership of all unmarked
 mute swans.

We all know Yeats's poem about the Coole wild swans,
but do you know Tennyson's "The Dying Swan" or Teasdale's
 "Swans"?

> So, Solonche, how long will you be a whistling swan?
> Enough whistling. My lips are dry. I'm now a mute swan.

Wolf

Old English *wulf,* of Germanic origin; related to Dutch *wolf* and
 German *Wolf,*
from Indo-European root shared by Latin *lupus* and Greek *lukos.*

In Mongolia, the symbol for good luck is the wolf.
In 1927 the Louveterie (special hunting force) killed the last
 French wolf.

In 1500, the English killed the last English wolf.
For fear of revenge, the Cherokee Indians did not hunt wolves.

In Europe in the 1600s, hundreds of people were executed as
 werewolves.
Anton Chekhov: "A wicked canary is better than a pious wolf."

No. 210 in the *Perry Index of Aesop's Fables* is "The Boy Who
 Cried Wolf."
The human wrist is called the joint of the wolf.

Inuits and nomadic Turks say the first man married a she-wolf.
Chinese call the star Sirius the Celestial Wolf.

    So, Solonche, do you have another howl for us?
    Yes, one more howl for you, in Latin: *Homo hominis lupus.*

Beard

From Middle English *berd, bard, bærd,* from Old English *beard,*
from Proto-West Germanic *bard*, from Proto-Germanic *bardaz.*

A French folktale from 1698 is "The Story of Blue Beard."
A restaurant and bar in downtown Indianapolis is *Bluebeard.*

The pirate Bluebeard is often confused with the pirate Blackbeard.
Humor and irony mark Kurt Vonnegut's novel (1987) *Bluebeard.*

In Islam and Sikhism, to be observant, a man must have a beard.
Dihydrotestosterone is the chemical responsible for the beard.

Science concludes that women are more attracted to men with
    beards.
Mesopotamian civilizations devoted great care to oiling and
    dressing their beards.

In India, in payment of a debt, a man may pledge his beard.
In Greece, a common form of entreaty was to touch the beard.

    So, Solonche, will you grow out your beard?
    Yes and no. Read my funny poem, "To My Beard."

Letter

From Middle English *letter,* lettre, from Old French letre,
from Latin littera ("*letter* of the alphabet"; in plural, "epistle").

The English alphabet consists of 26 letters.
With these, you can write 26 times 26 times 26 letters.

A letter in which the writer asks for money is called a begging letter.
A letter from a girlfriend to a soldier is called a Dear John letter.

The Persian Queen Atossa in around 500 BC sent the first ever handwritten letter.
Lincoln grew a beard at the urging of an 11-year-old girl's letter.

Lewis Carroll: "The proper definition of a man is an animal that writes letters."
Kafka gave his letter to his father to his mother who didn't pass on the letter.

Siegfried Sassoon, Martin Luther King, Jr., and Emile Zola wrote famous open letters.
In high school I played volleyball for which I earned a letter.

> So, Solonche, are you going to mail this "Letter-Ghazal" letter?
> No. If I did it would end up in the office of the dead letters.

Bridge

From Middle English *brigge,* from Old English *brycġ* ("bridge"), from Proto-Germanic *brugjō, brugjǭ* ("bridge").

The world's longest span (Japan, 2019) is the Akashi Kaikyo Bridge.
A 10.4-foot span between Portugal and Spain is the shortest international bridge.

Between Midgard and Asgard in Norse mythology is the Rainbow Bridge.
On the Isle of Man, greet the fairies as you cross the Fairy Bridge.

Sraosha, Mithra, and Rashnu are the guardians of the Chinvat Bridge.
In Taoism the entrance and exit to the underworld is the Hopeless Bridge.

The 22-mile Hangzhou Bay Bridge is the world's longest ocean-crossing bridge.
Robert Taylor and Vivien Leigh starred in the 1940 movie *Waterloo Bridge.*

Another English bridge used prominently in film is the Westminster Bridge.
The world's busiest bridge (104 million/year) is the George Washington Bridge.

> So, Solonche, any advice for life's upcoming bridges?
> I'll cross first and then burn after me, all those bridges.

Woman

Old English *wīfmon, -man,* a formation peculiar to English, the ancient word being *wife*.
Morning Blessings: "Blessed are you, Lord our *God*, who has *not* made me a *woman*."

There are two Hollywood movies (2009 and 2014) called *The Other Woman*.
Jean-Luc Godard directed a French film (1961) called *Une Femme Est Une Femme*.

Mary Wollstonecraft did not finish (1798) *Maria: Or, the Wrongs of Woman*.
In Greek mythology, Pandora is the first woman.

In Navajo mythology, Altsé asdzáá is the first woman.
In Act I, Scene ii, Hamlet says, "Frailty thy name is woman."

I often have wet dreams about Gal Gadot as Wonder Woman.
I often have wet dreams about Halle Berry as Catwoman.

Ditto Allison Hayes who starred (1958) in *The Attack of the 50' Woman*.
Ditto Daryl Hannah (especially!) as the remade (1993) 50 foot woman.

> So, Solonche, be serious for once. Who's your favorite woman?
> I'll be serious just this once. Emily Dickinson's my favorite woman.

Face

From Middle English *face,* from Old French *face,* from Vulgar Latin facia, from Latin faciēs.
James Cagney played Lon Chaney (1957) in *Man of a Thousand Faces.*

A Broadway musical (1927) and a movie (1957) are both called *Funny Face.*
Donald Duck played Hitler in an animated short (1943) called "Der Fuehrer's Face."

Ingrid Bergman stars in the Swedish film (1938) *A Woman's Face.*
Barbara Stanwyck stars in the Hollywood film (1933) *Baby Face.*

C.S. Lewis retells the Cupid and Psyche myth (1956) in *Till We Have Faces.*
Oscar Wilde: "A mask tells us more than a face."

O.W. Holmes: "Learn the sweet magic of a cheerful face."
Guinean Proverb: "For news of the heart ask the face."

Virgil: "Trust not too much to an enchanting face."
Abraham Lincoln: "Every man over forty is responsible for his face."

> So, Solonche, this is not a very good poem. Face it.
> Come out of there, you coward, and say that to my face.

Fame

From Middle English *fame,* from Old French *fame,* itself borrowed from Latin fāma.
Robert Burns: "Critics! Those cut-throat bandits in the paths of fame."

Sun Tzu: "A good commander is benevolent and unconcerned with fame."
George Santayana: "The highest form of vanity is love of fame."

H.D. Thoreau: "Even the best things are not equal to their fame."
Lord Byron: "Folly loves the martyrdom of fame."

Claudius: "Acquaintance lessens fame."
Pierre Corneille: "To myself alone do I owe my fame."

Whiting, Indiana is home (2018) to the Mascot Hall of Fame.
Rochester, New York is home (2015) to the world Video Game Hall of Fame.

London is home (2007) to the Dog Walk of Fame.
Las Vegas, Nevada is home (1990) to the Burlesque Hall of Fame.

>So, Solonche, what's your game?
>Like the man said, "The poet's food is love and fame."

Money

From Middle English *money,* moneie, borrowed from Old French moneie, from Latin monēta.
W.C. Fields: "A rich man is nothing but a poor man with money."

Don Marquis: "There is nothing so habit-forming as money."
In China, Tibet, and Mongolia until 1935, tea bricks were used as money.

In 2005 in Cameroon, bottle caps ($1 each) were used as money.
Since 2011 various countries have been using mobile phone minutes as money.

Gertrude Stein: "The thing that differentiates man from animals is money."
Plautus: "The day, water, sun, moon, night—I do not have to purchase these things with money."

Barack Obama: "I mean, I do think at a certain point you've made enough money."
Thomas Jefferson: "The glow of one warm thought is to me worth more than money."

Folk saying: "If your right palm itches, you will soon be getting some money."
Folk saying: "If your left palm itches, you will soon be paying out money."

>So, Solonche, what more do you have about the root of all evil, money?
>Nothing more than my two cents worth of money about money.

Sleep

Old English slæp from Proto-Germanic slepaz, from the root of
sleep (v).
John Milton (*Paradise Lost*): "What hath night to do with sleep?"

Homer (*The Odyssey*): "There is a time for many words, and there is also a time for sleep."
Shakespeare (*The Tempest*): "And our little life is rounded with a sleep."

Bogart and Bacall starred (1946) in *The Big Sleep*.
An animated short film (2002) is *Fish Never Sleep*.

Harold Lloyd's last film (1917) is *We Never Sleep*.
A rock song by Radiohead (2003) is "Go to Sleep."

During a new moon, you get better sleep while during a full moon worse sleep.
The average person can survive 2 weeks without H2O but only 10 days without sleep.

According to Guinness World Records, 449 hours is the longest period without sleep.
Hindus believe the god Vishnu dreamt of the universe while in his cosmic sleep.

> So, Solonche, anything else before you fall asleep?
> The Vishnu story makes sense to me but not unless I talk in my sleep.

Paper

Middle English: from Anglo-Norman French *papir,* from Latin *papyrus* "paper-reed."
In around 100 B.C., the Chinese invented paper.

One pine tree can produce about 80,500 sheets of paper.
Our "paper money" is composed of 75% cotton and 25% linen, not paper.

The *Acta diurna* ("daily acts") of ancient Rome was the forerunner of the newspaper.
"Notizie Scritte," printed in Venice in the year 1556, was the first monthly newspaper.

Yomiuri Shimbun of Japan is the world's largest circulation newspaper.
USA Today is the largest circulation American newspaper.

Origami is the Japanese art of folding paper.
Washi, made from the bark of the gampi tree, is the preferred paper.

About 16% of solid waste in landfills is paper.
Every year the average family uses 6 trees worth of paper.

> So, Solonche, want to keep putting pen to paper?
> No, another line won't make this ghazal worth the paper . . .

Nose

Old English *nosu,* of West Germanic origin; Dutch *neus, Nase,* Latin *nasus,* and Sanskrit *nāsā.*
The sound of your voice is shaped by your nose.

As we age, gravity sags and lengthens your nose.
When released, a sneeze comes out at 100 miles per hour from your nose.

Heinrich Heine: "Whatever tears one may shed, in the end one always blows one's nose."
Longfellow: "Joy, temperance, and repose, slam the door on the doctor's nose."

Woody Allen: "I am thankful for laughter, except when milk comes out of my nose."
Oscar Wilde: "There is nothing so difficult to marry as a large nose."

A human nose with a prominent bridge is known as an aquiline or Roman nose.
In Chinese tradition, the practice of Face Reading focuses on the nose.

In many cultures, a visit from a stranger is the meaning of an itchy nose.
A legendary character of Catalan mythology is The Man of The Noses or "home dels nassos."

> So, Solonche, how come you didn't mention your Jewish nose?
> Here goes. It's proven that penis size is directly correlated to the size of a man's nose.

Time

Old English tima "limited space of *time,*" from Proto-Germanic *timon.*
Planck time is the smallest standard of the scientific measurement of time.

We get more pleasure from overestimating time than underestimating time.
In 1836, John Belville, who worked at the Greenwich Observatory, began to sell (not a typo!) time.

The Sumerians were the first civilization to keep track of time.
Tolstoy: "The two most powerful warriors are patience and time."

Oscar Wilde: "Punctuality is the thief of time."
W.B. Yeats: "The innocent and the beautiful have no enemy but time."

A book I read (four times!) but did not understand is Stephen Hawking's *A Brief History of Time.*
A book I never read is James Baldwin's *The Fire Next Time.*

A great song by The Platters (1958) is "Twilight Time."
A movie with Fred Astaire and Ginger Rogers (1936) is *Swing Time.*

> So, Solonche, don't you still have a little time?
> Like the man said, time is relative, so I'll just take my own sweet time.

Star

Old English *steorra,* of Germanic origin; related to Dutch *ster,* German *Stern.*
Visible to the naked eye in the entire sky are 9096 stars.

The universe is comprised of about 200,000,000,000,000,000,000,000 stars.
Astronomers have identified 12 kinds (O, B, A, F, G, K, M, R, N, T, Y) of stars.

Red dwarfs comprise the majority of the stars.
Many cultures believe it is bad luck to point at a star.

In Britain it was believed that the soul of a new baby came on a shooting star.
Seneca: "There is no easy way from the earth to the stars."

Walt Whitman: "I believe a leaf of grass is no less than the journey-work of the stars."
Oscar Wilde: "We are all in the gutter, but some of us are looking at the stars."

A western movie with Henry Fonda (1957) is *The Tin Star.*
A song by Radiohead (1995) is *Black Star.*

> So, Solonche, do you believe that life is written in the stars?
> No, but it looks like this ghazal hitched its wagon to a star.

Corn

Middle English *corn,* Old English *corn,* Proto-West Germanic *korn,* Proto-Germanic *kurną.*
A new slang word in the US meaning weird, stupid, ugly, etc. is "corn."

British slang meaning "to get shot" is "to hold some corn."
Popcorn is a type of "flint" corn, a variant of maize or calico corn.

In the 1800s, as a substitute for expensive coffee, people used the cheaper corn.
A variety of field corn with a high starch content is Reid's yellow dent corn.

"One for the maggot, one for the crow, one for the cutworm, one to grow" is about corn.
Publilius Syrus: "Never thrust your own sickle into another's corn."

The Three Sisters is a Native American legend about beans, squash, and corn.
Demeter was the Greek goddess of agriculture, including corn.

In Aztec mythology, Centeōtl [senˈteoːt͡ɬ] is the god of maize.
For the Keresan people, the goddess Iyatiku plants bits of her heart that grow into fields of corn.

    So, Solonche, want to add one more row of corn?
    Sure, no problem. Here, underhand, so you can catch this can of corn.

Chair

Middle English: from Old French *chaiere,* from Latin *cathedra* from Greek *kathedra.*
The Egyptians invented the four-legged seat we know as the chair.

Alfred Porter Southwick (1826–1898) is credited with inventing the electric chair.
In 1790 an American dentist named Dr. Josiah Flagg invented the first dental chair.

As early as the 1600s, homes with children had highchairs.
Illustrated in the so-called *Löffelholz Codex* (1505) is a height-adjustable, swiveling chair.

The process that allowed wood to be bent with steam (1900) gave birth to the modern chair.
Michael Thonet, a German craftsman, created the first (1860) bentwood rocking chair.

Designed in France in 2017, The Skull Chair is the world's most expensive ($500,000) chair.
In some myths, Hephaestus, the Greek god of artisans, built himself a "wheeled chair."

The constellation Cassiopeia is so named because it resembles her torture chair.
The Chair of Forgetfulness was in Hades, and all memories were lost when you sat in the chair.

> So, Solonche, are you comfortable in that old chair?
> I'm not. That's why I'm done for the day and getting out of this chair.

Bed

Old English *bed, bedd* (noun), of Germanic origin; related to Dutch *bed* and German *Bett*.
The Egyptians invented the raised bed.

The Great Bed of Ware (1590) is a four-poster the size of two double beds.
Twenty-six butchers and their wives—a total of 52 people—spent the night in the Great Bed.

Many cultures have stories of monsters under the bed.
In former times, the left (sinister) side was the wrong side of the bed.

It is unlucky to leave your hat on the bed.
To reduce pain during childbirth, put a knife under the bed.

To frighten away demons, the British put round mirror medallions on their iron beds.
In Greek mythology, Procrustes stretched or cut off legs to force victims to fit into an iron bed.

Van Gogh's bed at Arles may be the world's most famous bed.
Ambrose Bierce: "Dawn. When men of reason go to bed."

> So, Solonche, you look tired. Ready to go to bed?
> I have sciatica. I sleep on the floor, not in a bed.

Hair

Old English *hǣr,* of Germanic origin; related to Dutch *haar* and German *Haar.*
In ancient times, slaves were distinguished by their bobbed hair.

According to astrologers, during a full moon is the only time to cut your hair.
Omens say that you lose vitality by cutting your own hair.

In Russia, pregnant women never cut their hair.
In Ireland, a traveler had to turn around if he met a woman with red hair.

Assyrian nobility used heated iron bars to curl their hair.
Starting in 1300, ladies used lizard tallow and swallow droppings for their hair.

Ancient Greek women used arsenic to give themselves blonde hair.
A long-running rock musical on Broadway (1967) was *Hair.*

Bette Davis: "I'd like to kiss ya, but I just washed my hair."
Mary Astor: "Men don't get smarter as they grow older; they just lose their hair."

> So, Solonche, are you going to do anything about all that gray hair?
> I'm just going to keep thanking my ancestors for this head full of gray hair.

Foot

Old English fot *"foot,"* from Proto-Germanic fōts.
Greek, Roman, Celtic, German, and Egyptian are the five shape types of the foot.

About 30% of the population lives with flat feet.
In India, it is a sign of bad luck if you have an itchy left foot.

For good luck, President Franklin Delano Roosevelt carried a rabbit's foot.
According to Wikifeet, the actress Emma Watson has the sexiest feet.

According to yournextshoes.com, Jennifer Hudson has the ugliest feet.
Mahatma Gandhi: "I will not let anyone walk through my mind with their dirty feet."

Samuel Beckett: "There's man all over for you, blaming on his boots the fault of his feet."
Keith Richards: "If you're going to kick authority in the teeth, you might as well use both feet."

Iambic pentameter is the most widely used English metrical foot.
Daniel Day Lewis won an Academy Award (1989) for a movie entitled *My Left Foot.*

> So, Solonche, one more step while you're still on your feet?
> Here, this is the last before I'm dead on my feet.

Hope

Late Old English *hopa* (noun,) *hopian* (verb,) of Germanic origin; related to Dutch *hoop*.
In Greek mythology, Elpis, the last item in Pandora's box, was the personification of hope.

A folktale from Somerset, Britain, is "The White Hind of Hope."
Martin Luther King, Jr.: "We must accept finite disappointment, but never lose infinite hope."

Alexandre Dumas: "All human wisdom is summed up in two words; wait and hope."
Robert Frost: "I always entertain great hopes."

Aristotle: "Youth is easily deceived because it is quick to hope."
George Washington Carver: "Where there is no vision, there is no hope."

Napoleon Bonaparte: "A leader is a dealer in hope."
Immanuel Kant: "What can I know? What ought I to do? What can I hope?"

Leslie Townes Hope (1903–2003) was the real name of Bob Hope.
An Italian movie (1952) is *Two Cents Worth of Hope.*

> So, Solonche, anything else to say on the subject of hope?
> Sorry. I've given up on that thing with feathers that rhymes with *nope.*

Work

Old English *weorc* (noun), *wyrcan* (verb), of Germanic origin; related to Dutch *werk* and German *Werk,* from an Indo-European root shared by Greek *ergon.*

New King James Version: "And on the seventh day God ended His work . . ."
Jan Lucassen is the author (2021) of the interesting book, *Story of Work.*

In 1911 domestic service was the largest part of women's work.
The Daughters of Liberty (1765) was the earliest society of women who worked.

In 1824, 100 Rhode Island textile weavers staged the first strike by women workers.
Harry Golden: "The only thing that overcomes hard luck is hard work."

John F. Kennedy: "The pay is good and I can walk to work."
Plato: "The beginning is the most important part of the work."

Horace: "Life grants nothing to us mortals without hard work."
My grandfather, Morris Karp, fought for the 40-hour week of work.

>So, Solonche, all finished with your hard work?
>Not at all. This is more play than work.

Wedding

From Middle English *wedding,* weddynge, from Old English
weddung.
In Mesopotamia in about 2350 B.C., is the first recorded evidence
of a wedding.

Couples in the Congo are forbidden to smile on the day of their
wedding.
Armenian couples balance bread on their shoulders during their
wedding.

In Ireland, the bride always keeps one foot on the floor when
dancing at the wedding.
Some Hindu women have to marry a tree before their real
wedding.

According to English folklore, Saturday is the worst day for a
wedding.
Wagner's "Bridal Chorus" from *Lohengrin* is not played at Jewish
weddings.

A tea ceremony is the same as an exchange of vows at a traditional
Chinese wedding.
When the groom is reluctant to marry the bride, it's called a
shotgun wedding.

A popular movie (2002) is *My Big Fat Greek Wedding.*
A tragedy by Federico Garcia Lorca (1932) is *Blood Wedding.*

>So, Solonche, do you remember your wedding?
>I remember getting drunk and falling asleep at my wedding.

Answer

Old English *andswaru* (noun), *andswarian* (verb), Germanic; from a base shared by swear.
Zora Neale Hurston: "There are years that ask questions and years that answer."

Voltaire: "Judge a man by his questions rather than his answers."
James Thurber: "It is better to know some of the questions than all of the answers."

Nietzsche: "We hear only those questions for which we are in a position to find answers."
Edward Abbey: "Not all questions can be answered."

Harmik Vaishnav: "Everyone wants answers but nobody wants to answer."
W.C. Fields: "It ain't what they call you, it's what you answer to."

Douglas Adams: "I refuse to answer that question on the grounds that I don't know the answer."
Ruskin: "To be able to ask a question clearly is two-thirds of the way to getting it answered."

A song on the album *Still Waters Run Deep* (1970) by the Four Tops is "Love Is the Answer."
An Israeli film (1955) about the 1948 Arab-Israeli War is *Hill 24 Doesn't Answer.*

> So, Solonche, are there any more answers?
> Only if a question spoken with authority can it be considered an answer.

Journey

Middle English: from Old French *jornee* day, a day's travel, a day's work.
A prominent theme in narratology and mythology is the "Hero's Journey."

Jonah and Odysseus are examples of those who go on heroes' journeys.
The films *The Matrix* and *Spider-Man* followed the same formula of the Hero's Journey.

A popular Disney film (1963) about a trio of pets is *The Incredible Journey.*
A documentary film (2005) about heavy metal music is *Metal: A Headbanger's Journey.*

A comedy movie (1991) with Keanu Reeves is *Bill & Ted's Bogus Journey.*
A documentary (2019) about the 1977 space mission is *Voyager: The Never-Ending Journey.*

A so-so song (1966) by Frank Sinatra is "Sentimental Journey."
A great blues song (1952) by Fats Domino is "Long Lonesome Journey."

James Brown: "Thank God for the journey."
Walt Whitman ("Song of Myself"): "I tramp a perpetual journey."

> So, Solonche, are you ready to end your journey?
> Yes, I've completed my day's work, my jornee.

Truth

From Old English tríewþ, tréowþ, trýwþ, Middle English trewþe, Old High German triuwida.
Henry David Thoreau: "Rather than love, than money, than fame, give me truth."

Pablo Picasso: "Art is the lie that enables us to realize the truth."
Lao Tzu (*Tao Te Ching*): "The truth is not always beautiful, nor beautiful words the truth."

Walt Whitman: "Whatever satisfies the soul is truth."
Gautama Buddha: "Three things cannot hide for long: the Moon, the Sun and the Truth."

Jean Paul Sartre: "Like all dreamers I confuse disenchantment with truth."
Plato: "You should not honor men more than truth."

A Hollywood comedy film (1937) starring Cary Grant and Irene Dunn is *The Awful Truth*.
A British film comedy (1957) starring Peter Sellers is *The Naked Truth*.

A documentary (2006) with Al Gore about climate change is *An Inconvenient Truth*.
A protest song (1971) by John Lennon is "Gimme Some Truth."

    So, Solonche, do you believe that beauty is truth?
    I believe that beauty is beauty, and that's the truth.

Nonsense

From non- ("no, none, lack of") + sense, from c. 1610. Compare the similar West Frisian ûnsin.
Joseph Addison: "Nothing is capable of being well set to music that is not nonsense."

Vladimir Nabokov: "The evolution of sense is, in a sense, the evolution of nonsense."
Alice: "If I had a world of my own, everything would be nonsense."

Bodhidharma: "Buddhas don't practice nonsense."
Mahatma Gandhi: "Well, India is a country of nonsense."

Edward Lear's *Book of Nonsense* (1846 and 1887) is the best-known book of nonsense.
College Student: "I hold Shakespeare ascribes meaning to Nonsense . . ."

In England, the phrase "All my eye and Betty Martin!" (1780s) meant nonsense.
In Australia, the phrase "Flemington confetti" (1920s) was a synonym for worthless nonsense.

"Moonshine on the water" is one of the earliest phrases on record (1468) meaning nonsense.
Charles Dickens used a version of "Gammon and spinach" as a synonym for nonsense.

> So, Solonche, what is your favorite nonsense?
> That's easy. The Marx Brothers are my favorite nonsense.

Mask

Mid 16th century: from French *masque*, from Italian *maschera*,
from medieval Latin *masca*.
Seven thousand B.C. is the date of the oldest found mask.

To filter mercuric sulfide dust, Pliny the Elder (23–79 CE) used
animal-bladder skins as masks.
Ancient Aztecs covered the faces of the dead with copper and gold
masks.

As a means of discipline, many cultures used admonitory masks.
To frighten their enemy, Japanese samurai used grimacing *menpō*,
or half masks.

In ancient Greece, worshippers of Dionysus wore white linen
masks.
In *The Great God Brown* (1926), Eugene O'Neill made striking
use of masks.

Friedrich Nietzsche: "Every profound spirit needs a mask."
Victor Hugo: "Virtue has a veil, vice a mask."

An acclaimed film directed by Peter Bogdanovich (1985) is *Mask*.
A horror film (1997) whose title I dare you say ten times fast is
Wax Mask.

> So, Solonche, are you ready to take off your poet's mask?
> Fooled you. I couldn't find it, so I've been wearing my
> masked poet's mask.

Light

Old English *lēoht, līht* Germanic from Indo-European root shared
   by Greek *leukos* and Latin *lux.*
King: *(Hamlet,* Act III, Scene ii) "Give me some light."

Victor Hugo: "To love beauty is to see light."
Theodore Roethke: "Deep in their roots, all flowers keep the light."

In a vacuum, 186,282.4 miles per second is the speed of light.
In the oceans, bioluminescence is the largest source of light.

Humans glow, too, but our eyes cannot detect the very weak light.
English astronomer John Herschel coined the term "photography,"
   which means "writing with light."

There is an English law called the 'Right to Light.'
To reduce crime rates in Scotland, blue bulbs are used in the street
   lights.

Crossed wires in the brain cause some people to sneeze in a bright
   light.
A great film (1963) by Ingmar Bergman is *Winter Light.*

     So, Solonche, have you finally seen the light?
     Yes, I'm now going to turn off the light.

Owl

Old English *ūle,* of Germanic origin; related to Dutch *uil* and German *Eule,* from the bird's call.
In 30,000-year-old cave paintings in France there are pictures of owls.

After banishing the crow, Athena's favorite bird was The Little Owl.
Before its defeat at Charrhea, the Roman Army was warned of impending disaster by an owl

Among early English folk cures, alcoholism was treated with the egg of an owl.
William Wordsworth's favorite "bird of doom" was the barn owl.

Apache Indians believed their death was approaching if they dreamed of an owl.
Lenape Indians believed it would become their guardian if they dreamed of an owl.

The most silent flier of any bird is the owl.
The world's smallest owl (southwestern United States and Mexico) is the elf owl.

The Blakiston fish owl (Asia) is the world's largest owl.
The eyes can make up to 3% (in humans it's 0.0003) of the entire body weight of an owl.

> So, Solonche, is it true that your neighbors are a pair of barred owls?
> Yes, it's true, which is why I really give a hoot about owls.

Wheel

Old English hweol, hweogol *"wheel,"* from Proto-Germanic hwewlaz.
In Greek mythology, Zeus ordered Hermes to bind Ixion to a fiery wheel.

The symbol on the national flag of India is the Dharma Chakra, the Eight-Spoked Wheel.
Taranis, the "Thunderer," was a Celtic storm god, symbolized by a sacred chariot wheel.

In the 4th century B.C., the Sumerians invented the wheel first used as a potter's wheel.
Four thousand B.C. is our first reference to a vertical water wheel.

Telephone, the fastest steamboat of its time (1884) was a sternwheeler.
George Washington Gale Ferris Jr. (1893) built the first Ferris wheel.

Aesop: "Put your shoulder to the wheel."
Susan B. Anthony: "I stand and rejoice every time I see a woman ride by on a wheel."

Danish Proverb: "When fortune's chariot rolls easily, envy and shame cling to the wheels."
A horror movie (1999) is *Hot Wax Zombies on Wheels.*

> So, Solonche, how much longer are you going to try to reinvent the wheel?
> After that disaster, I'm done spinning my wheels.

Bell

Early 14c., apparently from Old English bylgan "to bellow," originally of cows and bulls.
Traced to the Yangshao culture of Neolithic China, the earliest bells were pottery bells.

For 3000 years, metallurgists have used bronze (4:1 copper and tin) for making bells.
Weighing over 300 tons, The Great Bell of Dhammazedi was the world's largest bell.

Christian churches in around 400AD authorized the use of bells.
A true Cockney is someone who is born within the sound (six miles) of Bow Bells.

Signifying the original 101 scholars of Oxford, Christ Church rings 101 times its Old Tom bell.
The most famous American bell is The Liberty Bell.

Dutch Proverb: "Great fools must have great bells."
Spanish Proverb: "He who has lost his oxen is always hearing bells."

Clifton Webb stars in the comedy film (1951) *Mr. Belvedere Rings the Bell.*
You can hear the great Mahalia Jackson sing live at Newport (1958) "Rusty Bell."

>So, Solonche, got any more tolling of the bells?
>Ding, ding, ding, ding, ding . . . saved by the bell.

Fool

From Middle English fole ("*fool*"), from Old French fol, from Latin follis.
Known for breaking wind, Roland the Farter was King Henry II's fool.

Sexton, Will, and Jane, learning disabled adults, were Henry VIII's "natural fools."
Dogberry, Bottom, Trinculo, Falstaff, Feste, and Lear are famous Shakespearean fools.

Steve Martin, Kevin Kline, Peter Sellers, Charlie Chaplin, and Jim Carrey played film fools.
A hit song (1958) by Ricky Nelson is "Poor Little Fool."

A bluesy cut from the Grateful Dead's seventh album (1974) is "Ship of Fools."
Outselling every other American novel of 1962 was Katherine Anne Porter's *Ship of Fools.*

Molière: "A learned fool is more of a fool than an ignorant fool."
Mae West: "He who hesitates is a damned fool."

Philip K. Dick: "Many men talk like philosophers and live like fools."
Diogenes: "There is only a finger's difference between a wise man and a fool."

> So, Solonche, haven't you spent enough time around all these fools?
> Yeah, enough tomfoolery already. No more fooling around. No fooling.

Laugh(ter)

Old English *hlæhhan, hliehhan,* of Germanic origin; related to Dutch and German *lichen.*
Francoise Sagan: "To jealousy, nothing is more frightful than laughter."

Andrew Carnegie: "There is little success where there is little laughter."
Mark Twain: "The human race has only one really effective weapon and that is laughter."

Friedrich Nietzsche: "Not by wrath does one kill, but by laughter."
Chinese Proverb: "You will never be punished for making people die of laughter."

Lenny Bruce: "The only honest art form is laughter."
Catullus: "Nothing is more silly than silly laughter."

As opposed to when alone, people in the presence of others are 30 times more likely to laugh.
Plato thought the misfortunes of others are what make people laugh.

Freud thought that we release pent-up nervous energy or let off steam by laughing.
A recent theory says that the incongruity of expectation and reality causes laughter.

> So, Solonche, all set for the last laugh?
> Sure am, and the last laugh, as we all know, is always the best laugh.

Shit

From Old English, having the nouns scite (dung, attested only in place names) and scitte.
Gastroenterologists agree that it is not necessary to take a daily shit.

Mel Brooks: "I've been accused of vulgarity. I say that's bullshit."
Ernest Hemingway: "The first draft of anything is shit."

Before returning to Earth, Neil Armstrong left on the moon four bags of shit.
For survival reasons, we have evolved to hate the smell of shit.

Sloths leave their trees for only one reason—to take a weekly shit.
About 85% of the white sand on beaches in Hawaii is made from parrot fish shit.

The Egyptians made birth control devices from honey and crocodile shit.
In 1995 a woman set the world record—26 feet—for the longest shit.

Stercobilin is the chemical that gives the color brown to shit.
The official music video (2003) of Marilyn Mason is "This Is the New Shit."

> So, Solonche, do you have time for your own new shit?
> This coffee works fast, so please excuse me while I hurry downstairs to shit.

Morning

Late 14c., a contraction of mid-13c. morwenynge, moregeninge, from morn, morewe.
Romanian Proverb: "The hen that cackles in the evening lays no eggs in the morning."

Palestinian Proverb: "You will not dare mistreat the face you see in the morning."
Goethe: "The mind is found most acute and most uneasy in the morning."

Meister Eckhart: "Be willing to be a beginner every single morning."
Umberto Eco: "I love the smell of book ink in the morning."

Lt. Col. Bill Kilgore: "I love the smell of napalm in the morning."
Jack Dempsey: "Tell him he can have my title, but I want it back in the morning."

Cyril Connolly: "No city should be too large for a man to walk out of in a morning."
Harlan Ellison: "I go to bed angry every night, and I get up angrier every morning."

A popular movie (1949) with Bing Crosby and Barry Fitzgerald is *Top o' the Morning.*
A classic song (1974) by Willie Nelson is "Bloody Mary Morning."

> So, Solonche, how's your morning?
> Read line four again 'cause I wrote this at 8 o'clock this morning.

Luck

During the 1480s, a loan from Low German, Dutch or Frisian luk.
Yiddish Proverb: "Parents can give their children everything except good luck."

F. Scott Fitzgerald: "Nothing is as obnoxious as other people's luck."
Scotch Proverb: "The de'il's bairns hae aye their daddy's luck."

Russian Proverb: "Do not be born good or handsome, but be born lucky."
Serena Williams bounces the tennis ball five times before serving for luck.

On New Year's Eve, Spaniards wear red underwear while eating 12 grapes for luck.
Men in Thailand wear a *palad khik,* or surrogate penis amulet, under their pants for luck.

A crime movie (2016) is *Flatbush Luck.*
Painting the interior of your home with green paint is considered unlucky.

Victorian superstition holds that displaying just red and white flowers is bad luck.
Irish legends say that an empty rocking chair in your home is bad luck.

    So, Solonche, aren't you pushing your luck?
    Nothing more to push. I'm just plumb out of luck.

Silence

Middle English: from Old French, from Latin *silentium,* from *silere* 'be silent.'

Edith Sitwell: "My personal hobbies are reading, listening to music, and silence."

Leonardo da Vinci: "Nothing strengthens authority so much as silence."

Adrienne Rich: "Lying is done with words, and also with silence."

e. e. cummings: "Most people are perfectly afraid of silence."

Pythagoras: "Be silent or let thy words be worth more than silence."

Marianne Moore: "The deepest feeling always shows itself in silence."

Franz Kafka (*The Castle*): "You misinterpret everything, even the silence."

A movie (1966) starring Dean Martin is *The Silencers.*

Simon and Garfunkel's song "The Sound of Silence" was originally "The Sounds of Silence."

Another song (2006) about silence is by the Goo Goo Dolls called "Feel the Silence."

A novel (2020) by Don De Lillo is *The Silence.*

>So, Solonche, speak up. Anything else to say about silence? Like the man said in the play's last pun, "The rest is silence."

Smoke

Old English *smoca* (noun), *smocian* (verb), from the Germanic base of *smēocan*.
Japanese legend says that enenras are divine beings of darkness and smoke.

In Irish mythology, the Tuatha Dé Danann are elves associated with mist and smoke.
Rudyard Kipling: "A woman is only a woman, but a good cigar is a smoke."

Oliver Wendell Holmes: "Lawyers spend a great deal of their time shoveling smoke."
Yul Brynner: "Now that I'm gone, I tell you, don't smoke."

A rock song by Johnny Winter (1944–2014) is "I Smell Smoke."
An album (2014) by Dolly Parton is *Blue Smoke*.

Kacey Musgraves' anthem song is "Blowin' Smoke."
An independent film (1995) with Harvey Keitel and William Hurt is *Smoke*.

A Tennessee Williams play (1948) that failed on Broadway is *Summer and Smoke*.
An American western movie (1952) is *Apache War Smoke*.

    So, Solonche, isn't there any fire in all this smoke?
    Nope. Read my ghazal on *fire*. This one has gone up in smoke.

Blood

Old English *blōd,* of Germanic origin; related to German *Blut* and Dutch *bloed.*
There are 150 billion red blood cells in one ounce of blood.

Every play by Shakespeare has at least once the word "blood."
Crustaceans, spiders, squid, octopuses, and some arthropods have blue blood.

Insects, including beetles and butterflies, have colorless or pale-yellowish blood.
The human body has about 0.2 milligrams of gold that is mostly found in the blood.

Ichor, the golden fluid in the veins of the Greek gods and toxic to mortals, is their blood.
In Egypt Ra (the Sun) was said to have originated from drops of blood.

In Norse mythology, the drink of the poets is mead mixed with Kvasir's blood.
Satchel Paige: "Avoid fried foods which angry up the blood."

One of Errol Flynn's greatest films (1935) is *Captain Blood.*
Truman Capote's best book (1966) is *In Cold Blood.*

> So, Solonche, are you really out for blood?
> Not really. All I'm out for is some of that Norse poet's mead-blood.

Ghost

From Middle English *gost, gast,* from Old English *gāst,* from Proto-West Germanic *gaist.*
The ghost of Hamlet's father is undoubtedly the most famous of all ghosts.

The Drury Lane Ghost, Bloody Mary, The Vanishing Hitchhiker are also famous ghosts.
Casper the Friendly Ghost and Slimer are the favorite children's ghosts.

The Flying Dutchman, a 17th century ship, is the world's best-known non-human ghost.
Italo Calvino: "The more enlightened our houses are, the more their walls ooze ghosts."

David Lowery: "I'm an atheist. I don't believe in the afterlife, but I do believe in ghosts."
Burmese Proverb: "The blind person never fears ghosts."

German Proverb: "Love, thieves, and fear, make ghosts."
An Abbott and Costello comedy (1941) is *Hold That Ghost.*

A horror film (1944) with Lon Chaney Jr. is *The Mummy's Ghost.*
Number 10 of The Cat Who series of books is *The Cat Who Talked to Ghosts.*

> So, Solonche, are you ready to give up the ghost?
> Yes, I'm so weak after all this hard work I must be as white as a ghost.

Peace

Middle English: from Old French *pais,* from Latin *pax, pac-* 'peace.'
For over 99.999% of its existence before homo sapiens, the world was at peace.

The historical period following the end of WW II to the present is known as "The Long Peace."
Since its birth in 1776, the United State has enjoyed only 17 years of peace.

D.H. Lawrence: "People always make war when they say they love peace."
Aristotle: "We make war that we may live in peace."

A John Knowles' novel and a film adaptation is *A Separate Peace.*
Abraham Lincoln: "Avoid popularity if you would have peace."

Buddha: "Better than a thousand hollow words is one word that brings peace."
The most famous novel by Leo Tolstoy that I never read is *War and Peace.*

Jean Henry Dunant and Frédéric Passy divided the first (1901) Nobel Prize for Peace.
Among many songs about ending war is Curtis Mayfield's (1971) "We Got to Have Peace."

> So, Solonche, have you, at long last, found peace?
> No, I'm not looking for peace, but I am at peace with peace.

Lightning

Late Old English, "lightning, flash of lightning," verbal noun from lightnen "make bright."
Lake Maracaibo, Venezuela, holds the record for the highest concentration of lightning.

Every year in the world there are 1,400,000,000 strikes of lightning.
About 2,000 people a year are killed by lightning.

The Greeks and Romans erected temples at sites struck by lightning.
The Navajo say that the wink in the Thunderbird's eye is a bolt of lightning.

Sicilian Proverb: "I'll believe the thunder when I see the lightning."
French Proverb: "Not every thunderclap is followed by lightning."

James Dickey: "A poet is someone who stands outside in the rain hoping to be struck by lightning."
In Malamud's novel, *The Natural,* Roy Hobbs fashions a bat from a tree struck by lightning.

From 1941 to 1945, Lockheed built 10,037 P-38 Lightnings.
A great blues song (1964) by Howlin' Wolf is "Smokestack Lightning."

> So, Solonche, how long are you going to stand out in the lightning?
> See line 9. I'm still hoping to be struck once by lightning.

Weather

From Middle English *weder, wedir,* from Old English *weder,* from Proto-West Germanic *wedr.*
Proverb: "If the new moon holds the old moon in her lap, fair weather."

Proverb: Bats flying around in the evening indicates fair weather.
An open or closed pinecone actually can tell you what's happening with the weather.

Dr. John Fletcher, writing in 1613, said women produce more urine in colder weather.
In Kentucky folklore, pigs whose spleens are at the front when they're killed means bad weather.

Horatio Nelson: "I cannot command winds and weather."
John Ruskin: "There is no such thing as bad weather, only different kinds of good weather."

George Eliot: "It is impossible, to me at least, to be poetical in cold weather."
Katherine Anne Porter: "Life is a game of piquet played in a bramble bush in very bad weather."

A great song (1941) recorded at least five times by Lena Horne is "Stormy Weather."
A Merrie Melodies animated short (1953) with Tweety and Sylvester is "Fowl Weather."

> So, Solonche, do you still want to predict the weather?
> No, I'm done. I'm feeling under the weather.

School

Old English *scōl, scolu,* via Latin from Greek *skholē*
Reinforced in Middle English by Old French *escole.*

The first public high school in America (1635) is The Boston Latin School.
Jefferson wanted taxpayer dollars—it didn't happen—to fund schools.

In 1954 the Supreme Court desegregated public schools.
Children get the most homework in Russian schools.

Kids in New Zealand and Australia are not required to wear shoes in school.
Everyone eats the same meal, which the students serve, in Japanese schools.

Einstein: "Education is what remains after one has forgotten what one has learned in school."
G.B. Shaw: "There is nothing on earth intended for innocent people so horrible as a school."

The earliest television preschool series (1952–1965) is *Ding Dong School.*
A sophomoric comedy (1986) starring Rodney Dangerfield is *Back to School.*

> So, Solonche, aren't you tired of going to school?
> Yes, I'm all ready to graduate from this boring boarding school.

Home

Old English *hām,* of Germanic origin; related to Dutch *heem* and German *Heim.*
Japanese Proverb: "Don't stay long when the husband is not at home."

Togolese Proverb: "Better a stupid wife than a mess at home."
Emily Dickinson: "Where thou art, that is home."

Basho: "Every day is a journey, and the journey itself is home."
Alfred Lord Tennyson: "A smile abroad is often a scowl at home."

Edward R. Murrow: "We cannot defend freedom abroad by deserting it at home."
W.C. Fields: "I never worry about being driven to drink; I just worry about being driven home."

A classic movie (1943) about a dog is *Lassie Come Home.*
Another classic movie (1972) about a dog is *Snoopy, Come Home.*

A classic song (1985) by Phil Collins is "Take Me Home."
An unusually long (11 minutes plus) song (1966) by the Rolling Stones is "Goin' Home."

> So, Solonche, are you feeling right at home?
> No. This ghazal has eaten me out of house and home.

Miracle

Middle English: via Old French from Latin *miraculum.*
In the *Anguttara Nikaya,* a book of the Buddha's sayings, there are
   three kinds of miracles.

In China, Confucianism in the strict sense has little room for
   miracles.
In Judaism, nearly everything that happens is a miracle.

Islam assumes, as a matter of course, that Allah (God) works
   miracles.
Unlike the Buddha and Muhammad, Jesus had an ambiguous
   attitude toward miracles.

Cicero said nothing happens unless it can happen; hence there are
   no miracles.
Walt Whitman: "Seeing, hearing, feeling, are miracles, and each
   part and tag of me is a miracle."

David Ben-Gurion: "In Israel, in order to be a realist you must
   believe in miracles."
Saudi Arabian Proverb: "Do not stand in a place of danger trusting
   in miracles."

The first successful recording act for Motown Records was
   Smokey Robinson and the Miracles.
Perhaps the greatest ever sports call (1980 Olympics) is "Do you
   believe in miracles?"

     So, Solonche, do you believe in miracles?
     No. I believe what Whitman believed—everything is one
       big, fat miracle.

About the Author

Nominated for the National Book Award and twice-nominated for the Pulitzer Prize, J.R. Solonche is the author of twenty-seven books of poetry and coauthor of another. He lives in the Hudson Valley.